ALPHABET SOUP

ABBIE ZABAR

Published in 1990 by Stewart, Tabori & Chang, Inc.
575 Broadway, New York, New York 10012

Library of Congress Cataloging-in-Publication Data

Zabar, Abbie.
  Alphabet soup / Abbie Zabar.
      p.   cm.
  Summary: Descriptions of twenty-six (one for each
letter of the alphabet) unfamiliar but everyday foods
from around the world, with drawings, anecdotes, and
histories. Includes couscous, rijsttafel, goulash, kebabs,
and Welsh rabbit.
   ISBN 1-55670-154-3 : $14.95
   1. Food——Juvenile literature. (1. Food. 2. Alphabet.)
I. Title.
TX355.Z33 1990
641——dc20

Distributed in the U.S. by Workman Publishing,
708 Broadway, New York, New York 10003
Distributed in Canada by Canadian Manda Group,
P.O. Box 920 Station U, Toronto, Ontario M8Z 5P9

Distributed in all other territories by
Little, Brown and Company, International Division
34 Beacon Street, Boston, Massachusetts 02108

Printed and bound by Toppan Printing Company Ltd., Tokyo, Japan

10 9 8 7 6 5 4 3 2 1

❊ To Everyone Who Helped Flavor The Soup ❊
Leslie Stoker, Mary Albi, Andy Stewart, Roy Finamore,
Diana Jones, Kathy Rosenbloom, Rebecca Davidson,
Charlotte Safir, Elizabeth Young, Gerry Carr, Alan Heller,
M. & Mme. Bonté, Yolanda Beltran, Richard Ellis,
Emelyn B. Rosen, Bram Tahiny, Kate, Emily, & Lucy Stamel-Frank,
Jerry Wilson & Timothy,
Thank You
❊

ALPHABET SOUP

is dedicated to a child named Banh,
her little brother, her mother, her father,
and her grandfather, who makes them all so proud.
He's chief of the village.

Their country is Mali,
an African nation bigger than California and Texas together
and totally landlocked.
Families live in thatched-roofed huts with mud walls;
cereal grasses are the staple food; and
women and children walk miles every day
just to haul drinkable water.
Imagine.

A is for **ANTIPASTO**   ahn-tee-PAHS-toe

B is for **BORSCHT**   BAWRSH

C is for **COUSCOUS**   KOOS-koos

D is for **DIM SUM**   DIHM-SUHM

E is for **EDAM**   AYE-dam

F is for **FOOL**   FOOL

G is for **GOULASH**   GEE-yahsh

H is for **HUITLACOCHE**   wee-tlah-KOH-chay

I is for **INDIAN PUDDING**   IN-dee-en · PUD-ding

J is for **JOHN DORY**   jon · DOOR-ee

K is for **KEBABS**   kuh-BOBZ

L is for **LADYFINGERS**   LAY-dee · FING-gurz

M is for **MATZO**   MAT-suh

N is for **NAAN**  NAHN

O is for **OMELETTE** OHM-lit

P is for **PRIMEURS** PRE-murz

Q is for **QUINCE** KWINSE

R is for **RIJST TAFEL** RRRihs-tah-ful

S is for **SUSHI** SOO-she

T is for **TARTE TATIN** tart-tah-TAN

U is for **UGLI** OOO-glee

V is for **VARK** VARK

W is for **WELSH RABBIT** welsh-RAB-it

X is for **X-RAY FISH** EKS-ray-fish

Y is for **YORKSHIRE PUDDING** YORK-shar-PUD-ding

Z is for **ZABAGLIONE** zah-bahl-YOH-nay

Picture a platter filled with anchovies, tuna, and sardines;
mussels, mushrooms, and mozzarella;
slices of prosciutto,
plus sausages, both hot and sweet;
black olives and green olives, wrinkly skinned and smooth,
some with pits, others with pimientos.
There are breadsticks and celery sticks,
grilled tomatoes, marinated artichokes,
maybe a couple of hard-boiled eggs.
It's a rainbow of foods, a harvest of flavors,
raw or cooked, and whatever's in season.
ANTIPASTO can pass for a banquet,
but, imagine, it's only the beginning of an Italian meal.

Russian grandmothers make a purple soup from beets and beef
that's filling and warming.
BORSCHT is a hearty brew, chock-ful as a stew
and ladled piping hot from the pot
during those long cold months of a Ukrainian winter.
But as the snow melts and weather warms up
the broth is served in a tall frosted glass
with a scoop of sour cream.
Imagine, when summer comes **BORSCHT** looks and tastes
refreshing as a strawberry soda
even though it's still a soup.

Imagine a food that can be eaten for breakfast
instead of cereal,
for dinner instead of macaroni,
and as dessert instead of rice pudding.
COUSCOUS is made from the same semolina as spaghetti
but is pressed into beads
small enough to be strung on a thread.
In Morocco it's served with a spicy meat stew
and politely eaten with the right-hand fingertips,
but in Egypt a mound of **COUSCOUS** is sweetened with sugar
and sprinkled with peanuts for a delicious dessert.

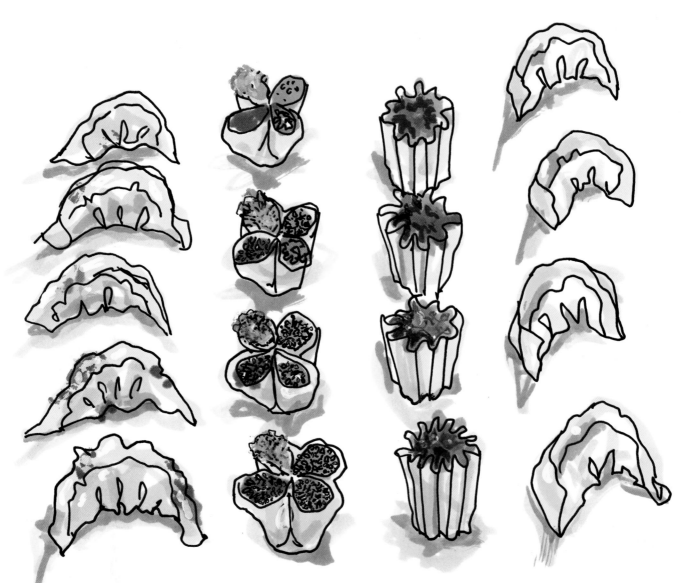

Lots of people
from all over the world
noodle around with noodle dough.
Italians roll out ravioli,
Jews create kreplach,
Poles prepare piroshki,
and the Chinese make dainty **DIM SUM.**
Imagine, they're all dumplings,
little packages of dough filled with
chopped meat, fish, vegetables, fruits, or sweets,
and a tasty way to stretch food from one meal to another.
But **DIM SUM** are made into many forms...
moon crescents, drawstring pouches, even blooming flowers.
It's like decoding a box of chocolates
and the shapes become a clue to what's inside.

Way back in the 1700s
those contented cows that grazed on Holland's green pastures
gave more milk than the Dutch could ever drink.
So before long,
clever monks from the town of Edam did some experimenting,
and pretty soon
many people from near and far were eating a cheese called **EDAM** .
It was mildly flavored,
easy to cut,
as round as a cannonball, and wrapped for export in a shell of hard red wax.
Imagine, at one time it was even rolled over cobblestone streets
from warehouses to nearby wharves
then shipped around the world.

Imagine a dish so simple
the English call it a **FOOL**.
But it was the ever-resourceful French
who made something similar with imperfect berries,
ones that were crushed or "foulées,"
who probably gave the English **FOOL** its name.

Just a fluff of whipped cream, sugar, and any soft fruit
that can be mashed with a spoon,
it was a favorite dessert with children
when guests were rag dolls and teddy bears,
as well as perfectly proper for grown-up parties
in the days before ice cream and way before freezers.

Back when Hungarian herdsmen prepared their meals
before setting off on a journey,
they would cut and cook cubes of meat
and then let them dry out in the sun.
Imagine, just like laundry.
At night they would unpack their knapsacks
and toss the dried beef, piece by piece,
into a heavy pot with some water,
cooking it over an open fire in the woods.

The stew is a meal in itself,
needing nothing more than very hard bread
to soak up the sauce.
It's now cooked on a stove
but still called **GOULASH**.

Mexicans have been growing and eating corn
for over five thousand years.
It's such an important crop that no part goes in the garbage.
Not even the **HUITLACOCHE**,
a silver-grey mold that creates swolen black kernels,
oozing a juice the color of ink.
Imagine eating a fungus,
usually just something growing on those vegetables
forgotten at the back of a refrigerator.
Delicious food is so often not what it seems;
but like mushrooms and truffles,
HUITLACOCHE is a sought-after delicacy...
a treat in hot soups, spread on tortillas, or even as a flavoring
for ice cream.

What's a steamy dessert that's as Yankee as Boston baked beans,
just about the same color,
and also cooks for eight hours in the oven?
It's an American dish, a New England favorite
made from molasses, cinnamon, eggs, milk, and
the cornmeal introduced to Colonists by the Indians.
Imagine something like warm melted gingerbread,
spicy and sweet
smooth and grainy
and, best of all,
cool and hot when topped with vanilla ice cream.
It's INDIAN PUDDING.

Imagine a fish with a man's name.
JOHN DORY has a head almost half the size of its body
and scales so small it looks nearly naked.
The sides are as flat as a pancake
and marked with a couple of black spots,
said to be St. Peter's fingerprints
when he scooped the fish from the sea
while guarding the Gates of Paradise.
From then on, it became the doorkeeper's fish,
and belonged to the "janitore"...
which sounded like Johnny-Dory...
but eventually **JOHN DORY.**

Long before vacuum-packing and picnic coolers,
food was often soaked in oils and spices.
After several days it was seasoned well
and well preserved.
Middle Eastern Arabs traveled with these marinated pieces
of lamb and mutton while going through the desert.
But when the caravans stopped for the night,
the spicy meat was removed from packs,
strung on reeds or twigs and grilled over an open fire,
just like toasted marshmallows.
No need for forks, knives, or spoons.

This may be the oldest form of cooking,
but imagine,
nowadays **KEBABS** are sold on the street
and still eaten on the run.

Imagine cookies known as Cat's Tongues,
Bull's Eyes, and Elephant's Ears.
Why there are even small cakes called
LADYFINGERS.
They are not too sugary, not too lemony, but a little bit spongy.
In France,
this boudoir biscuit surrounds fancy desserts
and is celebrated with champagne.
But when the British take their four o'clock tea,
pairs of **LADYFINGERS**
pressed back to back with a creamy filling
are passed around as sweet finger sandwiches.

Imagine a bread that's as flat as a piece of paper,
complete with rows of holes for tearing along the dotted lines.
MATZO is still eaten by Jews at Passover,
a reminder of their ancestors' hurried escape to freedom
when flour and water were quickly mixed
and baked under the hot desert sun.

But the dough never rested long enough to go sour,
and because it never fermented, it also never rose.
MATZO will always be an unleavened bread
that's thin, crispy, and noisy to eat.

Imagine a bread baked by hanging from walls
of a cylindrical clay oven that's sunk deep in the ground.
The elastic dough keeps stretching but never falls down,
and in less than sixty seconds it puffs up like a gigantic teardrop
that's fluffier than pancakes.

NAAN is a leavened bread from India with a slightly smoky flavor,
served warm straight out of the oven.
Small pieces are pulled off with the right-hand fingertips,
then wrapped around a morsel of food and popped into the mouth,
just like a mini-sandwich.

In France,
a couple of eggs are beaten 'til they're foamy as suds,
then poured into a buttered pan
that's as thin as a plate and sizzling hot.
The yellow circle is swirled with a fork,
quickly shuffled back and forth,
and finally folded over a flavorful filling.
Just imagine,
cheese **OMELETTES** for breakfast,
vegetable ones for lunch,
Some with chicken livers for dinner,
and even sweet **OMELETTES**
stuffed with strawberry jam for dessert.

Belgium is a flat little country
where crops grow on wee-sized plots
and vegetables are picked early and small.
Clever farmers quickly reseed their fields
and get two harvests to a season.

Imagine carrots, zucchini, broccoli, squashes,
and eggplants,
quite often no bigger than dolls' food
and all picked at the peak of flavor.
They're in their prime and called **PRIMEURS**.

Imagine a fruit as hard as a potato
that must be cooked before eating
and looks like an apple but isn't.
Perfect for pies and respectable with roast meats,
it grows from green to gold on a tree,
then glows pink when stewed in a pot.
QUINCE is a beautiful fruit with a dusty looking skin,
hard to chop and impossible to peel.

With all those contradictions there was bound to be trouble,
so it's no **QUINCE**-idence
that the golden apple in the Garden of Eden
might really have been a you-know-what.

Indonesians always believed in hospitality.
If the guest didn't like one dish,
there was sure to be something else.
The Dutch learned to expect this kind of princely service
when they ruled their faraway colony,
rightly called the Spice Islands.
Even today many Amsterdam restaurants cover a long table
with twenty to thirty bowls
filled with exotic tastes and aromas.
Imagine
sausages, chops, and barbecued kebabs . . .
crisp-fried peanuts and grated coconut patties . . .
some gherkins and cucumbers . . .
mango chutney and roast bananas . . .
flaky shredded-fish fritters, deep-fried shrimp wafers . . .
hot curries, even scrambled eggs.

And all served with an enormous bowl of white rice,
mellowing the spices,
adsorbing the liquids,
and providing a contrast,
while giving its name to this unique and elaborate colonial banquet.
RIJSTTAFEL is a "rice table" in Dutch.

Japan may be lean on meat,
but heaven knows, it's surrounded by waters rich in
tuna, sea urchin, octopus, carp, yellow tail, mackerel, crab,
shrimp, abalone, oysters, flounder, and squid.
Very fresh fish, never more than a few hours old,
is sliced and arranged into shapes,
almost too pretty to eat.
Imagine fish so fresh it's wrapped into rolls of
nutritious seaweed and rice
and eaten raw.
The Japanese call this **SUSHI**.

Two sisters, the Demoiselles Tatin,
ran a small hotel and very popular restaurant
across the street from a busy railway station.
They did all of the cooking, baking, and serving themselves.
But one night when things became too hectic,
the younger sister dropped an apple tart
on her way into the dining room.
Quickly, before anyone noticed,
she scooped it up... and ran back into the kitchen.
Phooey, the crust had broken
making it impossible to turn over again.
So she hid the cracks under a caramel glaze and called it

TARTE TATIN.

Imagine, the upside-down apple tart became an instant success and
is now a classic French dessert.

From the island of Jamaica comes a shriveled and deflated looking
football textured, mottled lime-green fruit.
Imagine something so pitifully homely on the outside, that
it's called **UGLI**.
But peel off that wrinkly skin,
which fits like a baggy suit of clothes,
and discover beautiful pulp, as bright as Caribbean sunshine.
It oozes a very delicious citrus juice,
sweeter than grapefruit and tangier than orange.
Not so ugly after all.

India's marketplaces are filled with fresh and dried spices,
glowing like jewels and often as rare.
Baskets and bins hold brilliant threads of orange saffron
that turn food yellow,
and the sapphire blue of indigo to wash clothes white.
There are shelled pistachio nuts as green as a parrot's feathers,
powdered red chilies as fine as ruby dust,
and mounds of pastel sweets decorated with **VARK**,
shiny as Christmas tree tinsel.
Imagine eating little desserts
iced with precious slivers of sparkling silver.

In America it's called a melted cheese sandwich,
in France a Croque Monsieur,
but it's a **WELSH RABBIT** in Wales.
Originally some Leicester cheese, red as rare meat,
was softened over a fire in a pot
with local ale and spices.
The mixture was then quickly poured over grilled toast
and substituted for a dinner of game
when hungry hunters returned empty-handed.
If topped with a poached egg
the **WELSH RABBIT** becomes a Golden Buck.
Imagine what a successful hunt it turned out to be,
especially for the rabbits and deer.

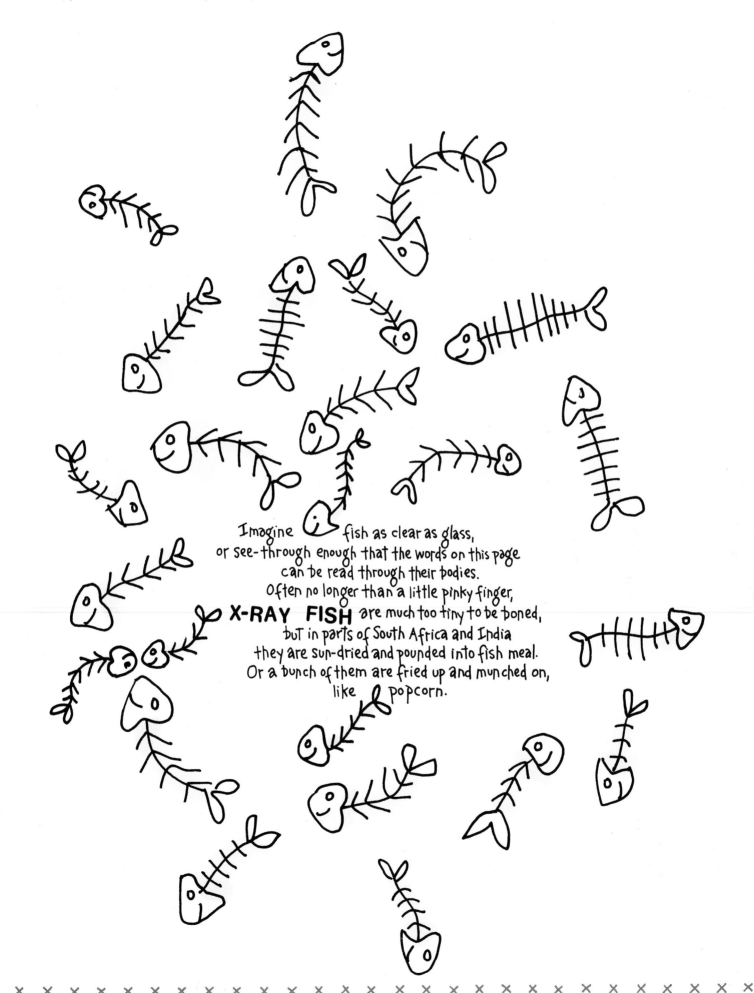

Imagine fish as clear as glass,
or see-through enough that the words on this page
can be read through their bodies.
Often no longer than a little pinky finger,
X-RAY FISH are much too tiny to be boned,
but in parts of South Africa and India
they are sun-dried and pounded into fish meal.
Or a bunch of them are fried up and munched on,
like popcorn.

YORKSHIRE PUDDING is not steamed or boiled
and may not be everyone's idea of pudding.
It's made of eggs, flour, and milk,
all poured into a roasting pan beneath a spit of meat.
Imagine a batter that bakes in hot drippings
and puffs up into a gigantic golden popover.
It's a true British pudding
served with rare roast beef at English Sunday dinner...
and there's no need for bread to sop up the gravy.

z z z z z z z z z z z z z z z z z z z z z z z z z z z z z z z z z z z

Now we all know about a cheese round enough to roll,
fungi that are feasts,
and tarts that are right side up when upside down.
But imagine an Italian dessert blowing up to triple its size
right before your eyes.
ZABAGLIONE is just a mixture of a yolk,
a yolk, a yolk, and still another yolk,
a little bit of sugar, and a dash of coffee or Marsala wine,
all quickly wisked over heat
to become as plump as a pillow.
It's the perfect ending to a meal
and the beginning of sweet dreams.

z z z z z z z z z z z z z z z z z z z z z z z z z z z z z z z z z z z z z